Poetic Meditations on Selected Scripture

Poetic Meditations on Selected Scripture

A Thirty-Day Devotional

JOHN P. DAVIS

foreword by Stephen M. Davis

RESOURCE *Publications* • Eugene, Oregon

POETIC MEDITATIONS ON SELECTED SCRIPTURE
A Thirty-Day Devotional

Copyright © 2021 John P. Davis. All rights reserved. Except for brief quotations in critical publications or reviews, no part of this book may be reproduced in any manner without prior written permission from the publisher. Write: Permissions, Wipf and Stock Publishers, 199 W. 8th Ave., Suite 3, Eugene, OR 97401.

Resource Publications
An Imprint of Wipf and Stock Publishers
199 W. 8th Ave., Suite 3
Eugene, OR 97401

www.wipfandstock.com

PAPERBACK ISBN: 978-1-7252-9864-4
HARDCOVER ISBN: 978-1-7252-9865-1
EBOOK ISBN: 978-1-7252-9866-8

04/05/21

Contents

Foreword by Stephen M. Davis	vii
Introduction	ix
Day One—Psalm 40:6	1
Day Two—Psalm 51	3
Day Three—Psalm 63	5
Day Four—Mark 2:22–38	7
Day Five—Mark 3:22–30	9
Day Six—Mark 3:31-35	11
Day Seven—Mark 4:3–20	13
Day Eight—Mark 7:2–23	15
Day Nine—Mark 8:31–35	18
Day Ten—Mark 9:1–13	20
Day Eleven—Mark 10:42-45	22
Day Twelve—Mark 11:12–25	24
Day Thirteen—Mark 12:18–27	27
Day Fourteen—Mark 12:41–44	30
Day Fifteen—Mark 13:1–13	33
Day Sixteen—Mark 13:32–37	35
Day Seventeen—Mark 14:22–26	38
Day Eighteen—Luke 2:10	40
Day Nineteen—Luke 19:41–44	43
Day Twenty—John 1:1–20	46

Contents

Day Twenty-One—John 3:16	48
Day Twenty-Two—John 5	50
Day Twenty-Three—John 9	53
Day Twenty-Four—Acts 1:15–26	56
Day Twenty-Five—Acts 2:22–38	59
Day Twenty-Six—Acts 3:12–26	62
Day Twenty-Seven—Acts 5:29–31	65
Day Twenty-Eight—Acts 15:1–21	68
Day Twenty-Nine—Romans 1:1–7	71
Day Thirty—Romans 6:23	73

Foreword

Many people who know John might be surprised that he has written a book of poems. John is many things as a pastor and theologian, but a poet? Who and what comes to your mind when you think of a poet—Longfellow, Whitman, Donne, Poe, Shakespeare, Dickinson? You may recall some well-known lines—"Tomorrow, and tomorrow, and tomorrow, Creeps in this petty pace from day to day..." (Shakespeare), or "Quoth the Raven 'Nevermore'" (Poe).

Poetry speaks to our hearts in a way that narrative cannot. Our inner being is touched and moved, at times to joy or tears, with the sublimity of words thoughtfully and exquisitely crafted to reflect an experience or a longing. Poems may stir our imagination and move us in our emotions. Some poems have a mystical quality which allow us to contemplate the finitude, frailty, and futility of our human existence, without providing hope of deliverance. Other poems have a transcendent excellence which points us toward the majesty and goodness of the Creator God and to the cross of His Son as God's response to redeem fallen humanity. We are moved beyond our little world of self-centered existence in order to ponder life as it was meant to be before sin entered the world, life as it is in a broken world of despair, and the glorious promises of God for the future re-creation and the establishment of His eternal kingdom.

Enter John the poet, who has no illusion of attaining the status or stature of the aforementioned poets. As a tattooed, weightlifting, Harley-Davidson enthusiast, John does not quite fit the mold of most famous poets. There does not seem to be anything in his life,

Foreword

humanly speaking, which predisposed him to write poetry. Over the years John acquired multiple academic degrees to the point that we quip that he is educated beyond his intelligence. He has been preaching for over forty-five years and at some point began writing poems during his sermon preparation which he would quote in his preaching. Perhaps we should not have been surprised that he had written the poems. And he may never have entertained the thought of publishing them. Yet his poems possess something of ultimate value that is often missing in celebrated verse. The poems are saturated with the gospel of Jesus Christ and the marvelous, mysterious grace of God which made him a child of God and transformed his life many years ago. John has drunk deeply from the gospel well and understands that every day he needs the gospel that he believed that day long ago for the first time.

This book is a welcome companion to his recent devotional book, *The Gospel in Genesis and the City*. Likewise, *Poetic Meditations* provides thirty days of selected Scripture reading with commentary and poems. In these poems John bares his soul and shares his life with its joys and sorrows, victories and defeats, hope and despair, and his utter confidence in the sustaining grace of God which saved him and will keep him until he arrives home in God's presence.

STEPHEN M. DAVIS, PHD
Elder, Grace Church Philly

Introduction

Since coming to Christ in 1970, I have loved and studied and taught the Scriptures. Fifty-years later that love is undiminished. Along the way, my love for poetry and lyrical forms came out of my love for the Bible. When I was in college, I was required to take a course on English Literature. I was a Bible major and a Greek minor, and I objected to the teacher about wasting my time studying literature and not the Bible. This very wise and patient teacher reminded me that a large portion of the Bible was poetry and I that if I wanted to learn the Bible, I would need to learn poetry. I am thankful for her gentle rebuke. Later in life, while working on my Th.M. at Westminster Theological Seminary, I had the joy of studying the Psalms and Proverbs under Dr. Bruce Waltke, increasing my understanding of and love for poetry.

I never thought I would write poetry. Perhaps there are some who will read what I've written and say that it is not really poetry. Nevertheless, I found myself often through my years of sermon preparation, reflecting and meditating on the text, then beginning to formulate in my mind lyrical summarizations of the sermons. I would write them down. Sometimes I would share them in a sermon. Mostly, I just collected them.

One day I shared some poetry with my brother Steve who then suggested that I publish them. Since I had already written a 30-day devotional on The Gospel in Genesis and in the City, he suggested I do something similar with the Scriptural texts and the poetry which came out of the texts. So here it is. I suggest that you

Introduction

read the portion of God's Word first, then the brief meditation, followed by the poetry.

May God speak to you and encourage you through His Word.

JOHN P. DAVIS

Day One—Psalm 40:6

Open My Ears, Lord

The image in our text is very forceful. It is as if David's head was a block of granite with eyes, nose, and mouth, but no ears. The ears have to be excavated—dug out. David speaks metaphorically. He already had physical ears, but he apparently wasn't hearing God speak. The implication of the context is that his being in the miry clay and slimy pit may have been due to his not listening to God.

The king may have picked up his copy of the scroll of the law scroll and read the words on the papyrus, but he wasn't hearing God speak. He may have gone to the tabernacle and listened to the priests read and expound on the Torah, but he wasn't hearing God speak. There was something wrong with his spiritual hearing. He needed God to dig new ears out of his granite skull.

Often the divine operation that God uses to excavate our ears is to allow us to fall into calamity or trouble that turns us to Christ in a new way with ears that have been opened. Your pain and hurt may be the excavating tool that the Spirit of God uses to open your ears. Ultimately, it is the gospel scalpel that excavates the granite heart so it can hear the word of God.

1. Hearing requires that you be made alive by having new life in Jesus Christ. Dead people do not hear.
2. Hearing requires access to the Words from God.
3. Hearing requires an ongoing work of the Spirit producing humility.
4. Hearing requires affections that listen for the voice of One who loves them.

Poetic Meditations on Selected Scripture

Our prayer today should be "Father, I have a granite skull. In your mercy, please dig new ears for me!

YOU HAVE DUG ME NEW EARS

I can see and touch and smell and taste
But there's a problem with my ears
His words seem cold as I read in haste
Only rarely am I brought to tears

In place of ears there's a granite block
Created of the hardness of my soul
The seed of his word bounces off this rock
A wounded heart cries to be whole

The Spirit of God can dig new ears
Enabling His words to touch the soul
His holy words bring joy and tears
His voice can make the wounded whole

Day Two—Psalm 51

Against you only have I sinned

The tendency of the world in which we live is to minimize and/or redefine sin. Of course, this is really nothing new. Satan used this approach in the garden with Eve. Satan defined sin differently than God did. Satan encouraged what God forbade. When God is removed from the scene, sin loses its ugliness and horror.

In some way this may be true of you. You may look back over this past year and find that you approved things in your life that God forbids, because you evaluated your life through the eyes of depraved society rather than through the eyes of a holy God. "Everybody does it."

This is essentially what David did. For one year, he had somehow justified murder and adultery, perhaps looking at these acts through the eyes of an oriental monarch who was above the laws of morality that governed others.

Let me briefly rehearse David's soap-opera-like story from 2 Samuel 11. His story includes at least the following:

- dereliction of duty
- lust and adultery
- cover-up, betrayal, and murder
- silence and apparent escape
- Nathan's indictment

Maybe it is not murder or adultery that you've allowed in your life. Perhaps it is tolerating ungodliness in your marriage; lust in your heart and mind; mistreatment and gossip toward others; stinginess toward God; self-righteousness that makes you hypercritical toward people; maybe it is laziness, racism, anger, etc.

Once the Holy Spirit convicted David of his sin and David looked at what he had done through the eyes of a Holy God, then he saw his sin differently and sought the mercy of God.

MY SIN

A rebel—in defiance of the King
A transgressor in so many things
Falling short of all that's right
Nothing hidden from his sight

Yet, kindness like a river flows
Great faithfulness his people know
A wayward child, a father's love
He brings cleansing from above

Blessed is the one who is forgiven
Grace and mercy flow from heaven
Sin's strong stain by blood made pure
Condemnation is no more

Come to Him to cleanse the heart
Joy renewed in the inward part
Guilt and sin, He drives away
Christ turns darkness into day

Day Three—Psalm 63

Reflections from the Desert

It is not uncommon to find oneself in the desert of life. There are many reasons why we end up in the desert. Sometimes living in the desert isn't our choice. David was driven there by a heartless act of family betrayal. Because we live in a fallen world it is inevitable that everyone will find himself "thirsty" in the desert from time to time.

- Marriage can become a desert filled with bitterness, harsh words, anger, and human misery.
- Family life can become a desert filled with disappointment and heartache.
- Spiritual life can become a desert where devotions, church, ministry become tasteless.
- The waning years of life when health is failing, friends are dying, can cause your soul to be dry and thirsty.
- A teenager's life may become a desert filled with hurt, misunderstanding, rejection, self-doubt.

We would rather avoid the desert, if we can. We prefer sun and sand with shade and a *pina colada* in hand and refreshing water in which to swim.

Notice again how the superscription reads: *When he was in the Desert of Judah.* As we begin to read the first couple lines of the poem, we see that another problem had come about. Not only was David "in the desert of Judah" but "the desert was in David." Just as the desert cried out for irrigation; David's soul needed water from

God. The real problem is not being in the desert but rather when the desert is in your soul. We can survive the deserts of life if the desert is not in our soul.

MY SOUL THIRSTS

My soul is thirsty,
Scorched by the fire of life
In a world singed by human strife
My soul is thirsty
Where barren desert surrounds
Fear and hopelessness abound
My soul is thirsty
Yet I hear my Savior say
Drink living water today
My soul is thirsty
I've found in Him a living spring
To Christ alone my soul will cling
Is your soul thirsty?
Come, taste, drink, be made whole
Quench the thirst of a yearning soul
Is your soul thirsty?
Come, drink of the living fountain
A river flows from Calvary's mountain

Day Four—Mark 2:22-38

Stealing the Joy of Others

Imagine this leisurely stroll through the wheat fields with Jesus on a sunny Sabbath in Galilee. The Sabbath was Israel's day of rest and a time for reflection on God's creation and His redemption. It was a day for joy and removal from the pressing obligations of six days of work.

This moment with Jesus is one of those rare carefree times to simply enjoy the walk and the world. As they walk, they pluck and eat the ripened wheat. They savor the moment, tasting fresh grain, leisurely strolling, and being with Jesus.

The Pharisees speak. Their words are like a thunderstorm on a quiet Mediterranean beach. Their accusation rings like that annoying wrong number at 2:00 in the morning when you've just reached a point of deep sleep. (Or for some of you it's like that startling clap of the preacher's hands awaking you from your sermon snooze).

The silence and quietude is broken: *"Look, why are they doing what is unlawful on the Sabbath?"* Suddenly, the wheat on the tongue no longer draws saliva. The sun seems to dim; legs labor to move on. The joy of that moment is swept away by the cloudburst of criticism.

What does God offer us through faith in the death and resurrection of Jesus Christ? Does the gospel take us from pleasure in sin to misery in Jesus? Is that our picture of the Christian life? Is the gospel a judge's gavel or the key to freedom? "If the son therefore shall make you free you will be free indeed."

Is the gospel a choker chain or a yoke that is easy and a burden that is light? Does the gospel call us to lives that are governed by what we think the Pharisees might say? Or, does the gospel call us to the loving and kind Lordship of Jesus Christ?

We aren't told what went through the disciples' minds that day as they witnessed this confrontation. They were in a quandary. On one hand they have the Pharisees who are the respected religious authority in 1st Century Palestine. On the other hand, they have Jesus who questions their authority.

I suspect that when the dispute was over, they plucked some grain, placed it on their tongue, salivated with joy, and went on walking with Jesus.

PICKING GRAIN WITH JESUS ON THE SABBATH

Walking with Jesus on a holy day
Plucking the grain along the way
A Heart filled with joy
A Mind that's at peace
Until I hear the Pharisees say,

You must be wrong
You're having fun
Those who are righteous
Don't live in the sun
They love the shadow
They fix upon gloom
They don't imagine
A fun-filled room

But Jesus speaks
With words so strong
"I am right and you are wrong"
I give life, and joy and peace
Freedom, love, and glad release
Follow me and you will see
I am better than the Pharisee.

Day Five—Mark 3:22–30

Lord, I am the Pharisee

In out text today, Jesus warns the Pharisees about having a cultural prejudice that blinds them from seeing God at work. The Pharisees demonized Jesus because of their prejudices. Do we not, as these teachers of the law, question and limit the power of God? Are we not motivated by similar prejudices that blind us from seeing God at work or from expecting God to powerfully work?

I understand the difficulty these teachers of the law have with Jesus' ministry. His method and results did not fit their religious and cultural paradigm. They could not see God working outside their box.

The work of the Spirit in Jesus Christ has a way of disturbing the ways we look at the world and the work of God. Remember how Jesus described the work of the Spirit in John 3:8. He said the Spirit's work is as a wind which blows where it pleases and though you may hear its sound you cannot tell from where it comes or where it is going. They were not willing to believe that Jesus was inaugurating the kingdom of God and that his power over Satan's kingdom demonstrated that the kingdom of God had come in Jesus. Jesus did not fit their conception of a Messiah. Their God worked only within their box. In their thinking, if Satan's kingdom was being invaded by the casting out of demons, then Satan himself must be behind it. Tragically, most of us are more comfortable with "God in a box."

Poetic Meditations on Selected Scripture

I AM A PHARISEE

A house filled with plunder
Lives torn asunder
Bondage and sin
Turmoil within
The Kingdom of Satan
The household of Satan

Jesus invades
The gates of Hades
Satan is bound
Freedom is found
Men are set free
For eternity

Who is this man
God or Satan
Should I believe
Forgiveness receive
Or shall I deny
I must not deny

Lord, help me to see
I'm a Pharisee
Eyes that are blind
A self-serving mind
Fearing the new
Not seeing you

Forgive me this hour
Show me your power
Rewrite my story
Show me your glory
Make holy my choice
To see and rejoice

Day Six—In the Family of Jesus

Mark 3:31–35

I imagine that like most families, it is pretty difficult to deny your family likeness. Though supernaturally conceived, Jesus was born of a woman, Mary, and somewhat bore her genetic likeness, as did his brothers. Perhaps the deep set of his eyes or the curved ridge of nose gave him away. Physical features identified him as the son of Mary and the brother of James, Joses, and Simon, Judas. Now he says, "Who are my mother and my brothers?" The answer is obvious (or should be), "Those outside the door to whom you bear likeness." I have five brothers all of whom bear some resemblance, either in the Davis eyes, or the smile, or the thickness of the wrists and hands. Were my five brothers to stand by my side this morning and someone were to ask, "Who are my brothers," the answer would be obvious.

What does Jesus mean in saying, "Who are my mother and my brothers?" He is moving the conversation to a deeper level. The intent of Jesus' question is this! Who really has a close family-like relationship with me? I imagine a throng of people pressing around Jesus in this home. Closest to him are the disciples who sit front and center drinking his words as the water of life. He looks at Peter, Andrew, James, and John, blue-eyed fisherman peeking through bearded and wrinkled sun-blackened faces. Here are my brothers! He looks at Mary Magdalene who once sold her body as a cheap commodity but who now presents it as holy and acceptable to the Lord. Here is my mother! His eyes fall on Matthew the cheating, traitorous tax collector that now sits at the feet of Jesus. Here is my brother!

Poetic Meditations on Selected Scripture

He looked around and then he said, "Here are my mother and my brothers!" As Jesus looked at the crowd, he saw in every face a redemption story. Every face provoked remembrance of an encounter between a lost person and One who came "to seek and to save the lost."

MY BROTHER LOOKED AT ME

Abandoned, forsaken, his eyes fall on me
"Brother you are, my family"
His smile of approval, my glad memory
I am his and he is mine, eternally

Does Jesus call you sister or brother?

He calls me brother, what can I say
His words calm my fear on a lonely day
He calls me brother, what do I feel
But comfort, peace, and joy that are real
He calls me brother, what shall I choose
To gain the world or my life to lose
He calls me brother, here's what I say
"Our Father's will, I shall obey
You are my brother, you are my friend
Brothers we are until the end"

Does Jesus call you sister or brother?

Does Jesus call me brother? Do I obey?
Is the path I'm walking his Father's way?
Does Jesus call me brother? Do I belong?
Is his father's will my guide for right and wrong?
Does Jesus call me brother? Am I his friend?
Can he count on me to serve him to the end?
Does Jesus call me brother? Yes, I see it in his eyes.
A glance, a smile assuring that I'm his prize
Does Jesus call me brother? I hear his loving voice
"Brother, you are, my friend in whom I rejoice."

Day Seven—Mark 4:3-20

The Sower, The Seed, The Soil

Jesus offers us a parable about a sower, seed, and soil. He uses a metaphor familiar to his hearers. The common approach to planting was to spread the seed on top of the ground then plow it under. So the farmer would widely distribute seed in a field that had varying possibilities. Some would fall on the path trodden down by those that followed the shortest distance through the field. Some would fall on soil that had a layer of rock lying just beneath the topsoil. Some would fall on ground that was infested with thorns and weeds. Most would fall on good ground. By the time the seed was plowed under the birds would already have eaten the seed on the path. The seed in the soil with the rock lying beneath would never really take root. The abundance of weeds would soon choke the seed in the weed-infested ground. The seed in good soil would bear fruit.

As he explains the parable to his disciples it becomes apparent that the Sower is Jesus, the soils are human hearts, and the seed is the gospel, the good news that kingdom of God has arrived in Jesus Christ.

If we read carefully, we see that the parable offers us a picture of the miraculous success of the gospel. There is a parallel between three failures and at least three successes—some 30, 60, and 100-fold. What is striking is the miraculous fruitfulness of the gospel. The parable is about the mysterious and miraculous growth of the kingdom. The seed of the gospel will triumph. The sowing doesn't reveal the success. The harvest does. A harvest of 10 to 1 was considered excellent; the average was 7.5 to 1. A harvest 30 to 1, or 60 to 1, or 100 to 1 is miraculous.

We are a people who walk by faith not by sight. We live in hope knowing that what we now see is not the complete picture. In the kingdom parables there is a focus on eschatology—the harvest at the end of the age reveals the true success of the gospel.

THE SOWER, THE SEED, THE SOIL

A heart that is hard or full of fear
May never hold the word of God dear
A heart that's full of envy and lust
Can not in the word of God trust
A heart must be soft and tender
One that's not a pretender
It must be courageous and strong
For the word of God to belong
A heart must be holy and free
If fruitful it will be.

God, fruitfulness is my desire
Let your word come as a fire
Like a hammer crush my heart of stone
Purged of weeds to love you alone

The gospel is the powerful seed
Penetrating to the deepest need
of human souls like hardened soil
becoming part of Satan's spoil
God's seed is powerful, you see
Preventing souls from tragedy
Bringing life from barrenness
Bearing fruits of righteousness

Day Eight—Mark 7:2-23

It's My Heart, LORD

Our failure to see our sin and to grapple with our depravity is primarily what incapacitates us from real ministry in a fallen world. The self-righteous masquerade that we parade for them is not convincing. Most non-believers may accept that we are forgiven but will not accept that we are nearly perfect.

I am not saying that we must become really sinful in order to be effective. I am saying that we already are sinful so let us make a big deal about God's grace.

Even the apostle Paul could cry out "oh wretched man that I am who shall deliver me from this body of death?" It is only when we see our sin clearly that we will love the gospel dearly.

The tragedy of the cross makes no sense if I do not see the horror of my sin. Why such suffering for the Son of God? Part of that answer is found as I look into my own soul?

Look into your own heart and see its horrid filth, then realize that Jesus, pure and holy, took all of that on himself to redeem you. This leads to praise.

Why did he suffer so?

- though mighty he hung in weakness for my sin
- though guiltless he hung in shame for my sin
- though beautiful he hung disfigured for my sin
- though victorious he hung defeated for my sin
- though loving he hung rejected for my sin

Why? For my sin. This is the gospel—"that Christ died for our sins according to the Scriptures, was buried, and rose again the third day according to the Scriptures."

It is only helpful to take a good look at your heart if it leads you to the cleansing gospel of Jesus Christ. To remain introspective is morbid—the gospel leads to forgiveness and resurrection—new life in Jesus Christ.

IT'S MY HEART, LORD

It's my heart, Lord, yes, my heart
Corrupt and filthy in the inner part
Secret admirer of all called—sin
A burning passion for evil within

It's my heart, Lord, yes, my heart
Greed and malice in the inner part
Envy, slander, deceit and folly
Far apart from all called holy

It's my heart, Lord, yes, my heart
Lewd, immoral in the inner part
Theft, murder, and adultery
Arrogance ruling within me

It's my heart, Lord, yes. My heart
It's who I am in the inner part
Unclean within, it's not the outside
I'm vile, unholy, full of pride

It's my heart, Lord, yes, my heart,
Cleanse me deep in the inner part
The blood of Christ can wash the soul
The blood of Christ can make me whole

It's my heart, Lord, yes, my heart
Through faith alone, a brand new start
Though warring now with latent sin
Assured in Christ the war to win

Day Eight—Mark 7:2-23

Take my heart, Lord, Take my heart
Cleanse me deep in the inner part
Conquer vice that lives within
Freed to love and not to sin

It's my heart, Lord, it's my heart
Life proceeds from the inner part
Wellspring of life is the heart indeed
To love Christ, it's greatest need

Day Nine—Mark 8:31-35

Take up the Cross

This is one of the three scenes in Mark where Jesus clearly announces His death. Imagine this scene with me. Peter has just confessed the Jesus is the Messiah, the long-awaited king and deliverer of the world. Now he hears Jesus talk about suffering, betrayal, and death. Jesus does not just talk about possibilities, but about necessities— *the Son of Man must suffer many things and be rejected. . .and be killed.*

Peter took him aside, "Jesus, we really have a good thing going. Crowds are thronging around you. It appears that your mission is succeeding. Let us not talk about suffering and death. People do not want to hear this! They want to hear the stuff that makes them feel good. This will hurt your PR. There is no way that we can market this stuff about suffering, rejection, and death."

I hope that we can see ourselves in Peter and not be too hard on him. I hope we can admit that our modern mindset is much more comfortable with silver and gold crosses than blood-soaked ones. We would much rather talk about Jesus the Good Shepherd than the Good Shepherd who lays down his life for his sheep. It's easier to talk about Christ the bread of life that satisfies the hungry soul than to discuss the implications of what it means for bread to be broken.

Do you ever, like Peter, want to rebuke God for devising such an unappealing plan of bringing life to a dying world? I still remember those frequent conversations with one of my friends who was repulsed by the message of the cross. He liked Jesus and would even

Day Nine—Mark 8:31-35

say that he accepted him, but he would add, "I cannot accept that God would allow His Son to suffer such a cruel and violent death. I did not ask him to die for me so why should I have to accept his death?"

On one hand, I empathize with his struggle. A blood-soaked cross is not an appealing symbol of victory. Why not a warrior's sword, or a clenched fist, or a hammer and sickle, or a flaming torch? Why a blood-soaked cross? When you answer that question and believe, you are on your way to a new life in Christ.

TAKE UP THE CROSS

To gain the world was once my goal
Though at the cost of losing my soul
The cross offended this sinful heart
Of Christ and grace wanting no part
Sin and pleasure beckoned me
Hating holiness and sovereignty

But Jesus' love pursued this rebel
Conquering sin and death and the devil
His blood-soaked cross summoned me
Offering grace and liberty
I've lost the world to gain my soul
To live for Christ is now my goal

Jesus, the cross I willingly bear
Your suffering, rejection, and death to share
No longer bent on preserving my soul
Living a life that you made whole
Unashamed I speak of your grace
The smile of approval upon your face

Day Ten—Mark 9:1–13

Is this the End of the World?

Popular Christian fiction, though often light on theology and heavy on speculation, promotes end-time thinking. There is a natural curiosity about knowing how it will all end. Is this the end? It could be, but may not be for 1000 years.

Continuing world events open the door for discussion about the end of the world. Are these events a precursor to the end? My reply is that there is no way to determine their significance regarding the end of the world but they are significant regarding the end of life. People die! People die in unexpected and tragic ways. People die! Some go to heaven; some go to hell. Yes, people die, for "it is appointed unto men once to die and after that the judgment."

What is significant about these events is that God has the attention of the living! And, hopefully these events will cause people to recognize the most significant eschatological event of human history, i.e., the death and resurrection of Jesus Christ. (You may wonder how an event that took place 2000 years ago can be the most significant event on God's prophetic timetable.)

It's more important to know why did Jesus die. God gets people's attention through cataclysmic events, but sinners come to salvation only through the gospel.

From Jesus' perspective, the most important end time happenings are not the sequence of cataclysmic events at the very end—but one end time event that has signaled that the end has come, i.e., the death and resurrection of Jesus Christ.

Day Ten—Mark 9:1-13

I'm afraid that we are often more interested in the sequence of events than in the significance of his suffering.

From Jesus' viewpoint, the most significant prophetic event is not the rise of Antichrist, or the opening of seals, or the blowing of trumpets, or the emptying of bowls. The most significant event that signals the end of the world is the cross of Jesus Christ and His resurrection.

When God judged your sin and mine in Jesus on the cross and when he brought him out of the grave on the third day, he signaled that now is the day of salvation. Now is the time of repentance. Judgment and redemption hinge on what we do with Jesus Christ.

IS THIS THE END OF THE WORLD?

Is this the end of the world? Does anyone really know?
When towers fall, buildings crumble, men run to and fro
Is this the end of the world? Is life coming to an end?
When scorching flames devour both a loved one and a friend
Is this the end of the world? Has God poured out His wrath?
Airplanes as bombs, veering off their paths

Is this the end of the world? What does Jesus say?
The end of the world began over 2000 years away
Towers fall, buildings crumble, men called to repent
To rescue them from eternal flames is the reason He was sent
Loved ones die and even friends pass into eternity
What they did with Christ determines where they will be

When towers fall and buildings crumble, look back to the cross
Remember that, for your salvation Jesus suffered loss
Though crashing planes and scorching flames seem in control
Be careful not to fear the things that can never touch your soul

The end of the world is NOW and has been for 2000 years
Through faith in Christ alone we move beyond our fears
Towers fall and buildings crumble, but this one thing stands true
Jesus died and rose again; He'll return to make all things new

Day Eleven—The Jesus Way to Greatness

Mark 10:42–45

Jesus doesn't diminish or rebuke the desire to be great. He simply shows that the measure of greatness in the kingdom differs from that in the world. Look at the two words that Jesus uses: "the rulers of the Gentiles lord it over them, and their high officials exercise authority over them."

Note that both of these verbs in the Greek have a prefix (*kata*—over) attached to it that indicates downward movement. Greatness in the world is a position from which you look down. Greatness in the world is concerned with power, superiority, advantage, predominance, domination, and control.

What is greatness in the world? By the world's measurement greatness is achieved through superior acts that distinguish you *above* others. How you get there isn't necessarily important.

The end, not the means, measures greatness in the world. Greatness focuses simply on that result—you are on top. Regardless of how one got there, what matters is that you somehow have the ability to "look down." You are on top!

How often we play king of the mountain, getting on top by knocking others down with criticism, faultfinding, gossip, destruction of reputation. I can always make myself look better than anyone by focusing on his or her sin or failure. This is the world's way. It's not the Jesus way to greatness. Jesus simply says, "the way to greatness is not through gaining position and power over others."

Day Eleven—The Jesus Way to Greatness

Greatness is not the view from the top but the view through the eyes of a servant asking, "How can I serve you in a way that attracts you to the kingdom of Jesus Christ?"

THE JESUS WAY TO GREATNESS

How can I serve you, is what I should ask.
Because helping others is a Christian task
How may I help you along your way?
Whatever the cost, I'm willing to pay.
Serving is what God calls me to do
He cared for me so I'll care for you

Why, you might ask, would you care for me?
It's because I was blind and now I see
I came to One who opened my eyes
Desperate was I, though well disguised
He looked past my mask and into my heart
He mended a life that was falling part

Christ gave his life and so must I
To my pride and my hate I'm willing to die
He offered forgiveness and new life too
He taught me to love; that's why—I serve you

Day Twelve—Mark 11:12-25

Forgiving Others

What is forgiveness? It is releasing the offender of any personal (not necessarily legal) liability toward you for what they have done to you. Forgiveness opens the door for reconciliation that leads to a new relationship.

When should I most likely think about forgiving? Anytime I want to pray! Jesus indicates that anytime we come to God in prayer we need forgiveness.

It is easy to forget our own sinfulness, isn't it? But every time we come boldly before the throne of grace in prayer, we come into the presence of one who alone is Holy. Like Isaiah, when we look upon God's holiness and see our sinfulness, we must cry out for God's mercy and forgiveness.

The failure to acknowledge and confess our own sinfulness is precisely the reason why we fail to forgive others. The knowledge of our own sinfulness and need of forgiveness provides the impetus to forgive others. Let us be honest with our own sin and need of forgiveness that we might be generous in forgiving others.

What shall I forgive? Everything! If you do not forgive, the only other option is bitterness and resentment. Someone has said that resentment is like drinking a cup of poison while waiting and hoping for the other person to die.

Why should I forgive? Because forgiving others keeps the door open for God to forgive me. Jesus isn't suggesting a meritorious act where "you do this and God will do this." Whatever God does for us is done for us in grace and mercy based solely on the merits of

Day Twelve—Mark 11:12-25

Jesus Christ. Jesus is simply pointing out the incongruity of seeking God's forgiveness for other sins while we are still committing the sin of not forgiving others. He is simply reminding us that one of the conditions of prayer is coming to God through Christ with a pure heart. Not forgiving others pollutes the heart.

TO FORGIVE OR NOT TO FORGIVE!

Like a sword your words pierced to my soul
Like a hammer your look brought a crushing blow
No words can describe the deep anguish within
My tears fail to show the heartbreak of sin

Like a late summer flower whose fragrance is gone
Though once a fresh spring, my heart's now a stone
The barrenness of winter has come for a day
Fruitless and stagnant is where I will stay

Should I forgive or shall I remain cold?
Is bitterness and anger the way to grow old?
Enslaved to my thoughts, a captive I'll be
Or is there a way for me to be free?

I see on the cross a pitiless form
Beaten, despised, His holy flesh torn
Blood on his brow, spit on his face
Unjustly, cruelly he hangs in my place

Their words call for hatred, anger, and more
His words do not seek to settle a score
He is the Christ and speaks what is true
Father, forgive them, they know not what they do.

Christ has forgiven and so must I
No matter how hurt, yet still I must try
When I forgive others, He then forgives me
That faultless and cleansed in prayer I might be.

Poetic Meditations on Selected Scripture

Yes, we have choice in how we'll grow old
Hearts like fresh springs or hearts that are cold
Late summer flowers or the fragrance of spring
The barrenness of winter or new life we bring

Day Thirteen—Mark 12:18-27

Answering Questions about Life after Death!

The Sadducees did not believe in the resurrection nor did they believe in angels. The Sadducees denied the separate existence of human souls. They taught that human souls die with the bodies. They held only to what they found clearly taught in the Books of Moses. They did not see life after death taught in those five books. And, even though Moses spoke of angelic beings, they explained them away as theophanies.

The Sadducees assumed that there is an irreconcilable conflict between what they knew Jesus believed about the resurrection on one hand and what they assumed he believed on the other hand about the continuing of marriage in heaven. The Sadducees knew that every good Jew believed in the Levirate law of marriage. This law said that if a Jewish man died and left a wife without children, then her brother-in-law must marry her so that she can bear a child who will carry on the name of the deceased husband (Deut. 25:5-10). There was a popular belief among Jews that there was a continuing of the marriage order in heaven. The Jews had mingled this popular belief with the biblical teaching of the resurrection.

They present a dilemma to Jesus for which they are sure there is no resolution. It is probably the kind of riddle that Sadducees would share with their children as they ridiculed those who believed in the resurrection.

Jesus does not shrink back from a confrontation. We are here talking about issues of life and death, for to deny the resurrection is to deny God himself. If he gave an eternal covenant to Abraham,

Isaac, and Jacob that was severed by their deaths, then His covenant word is useless.

We are not talking about minor points of doctrine that have no bearing on the gospel and the character of the Triune God. We are talking about issues of life and death.

Jesus doesn't surrender one bit of holy truth in order to continue the conversation with the Sadducees. He understands that there are some things that are antecedent to any logical discussion.

He presupposes the authority of Scripture. He makes two statements even knowing that they don't believe them: "When the dead rise" (they didn't believe in the resurrection, yet he assumes it as true) and "as the angels in heaven" (they didn't believe in angels, yet he assumes them as being real).

We should never give up truth for the sake of getting along!

LIFE AFTER DEATH

Is there life after death, who really knows?
Do all pass through dark tunnels where eternal light glows?
If I'm not really bad, is there a halfway house
Or will I be ashes if I've been a louse

Is there really a heaven and really a hell?
Will it be eternal fire or where all is well
One religion says yes and another says no,
When I breathe my last breath, where I will go?

How can I know which way is right?
When everyone claims to walk in some light
Is there only one truth that sets men free
Can I have peace about where I will be?

Shall I trust my soul to those who are dead
Or have faith in One who is risen, instead
Who created the world and gave me breath
Who speaks the truth about life after death?

Day Thirteen—Mark 12:18-27

The answer comes in a servant's form
From heaven to earth on a Christmas morn
To a cross, which seemed a tragedy
To an empty tomb shouting victory

His risen life has now become mine
The joy I now have will pass beyond time
Through faith in Christ I know I will be
Alive—both for time and eternity.

Day Fourteen—Mark 12:41-44

How much should I keep for myself?

This is one of a number of strategically placed stories in the gospel of Mark that sets forth unlikely people as models of discipleship, such as blind Bartimaeus and later a woman who anoints him with expensive oil at the house of Simon.

This story of the poor but generous widow is also strategically placed in this gospel, as an indictment of false religion, i.e. it indicts the covenant unfaithfulness of Israel and her leaders. It is a contrast of simple trusting faith with ostentatious religious hypocrisy.

It is a text that should make us uncomfortable because we often lay somewhere on the continuum between religious hypocrisy and simple trusting faith. We aspire to be the widow without quite getting there and often are like the Scribes and the insensitive rich.

In the end it causes us to be grateful for Christ's death and resurrection which forgives us and rescues us despite our failure to fully reject religious hypocrisy and our failure to fully experience simple trusting faith.

It is only the gospel that calls us and empowers us to seek the simple faith and faithfulness depicted in the giving of this woman.

Imagine this setting. Jesus places himself at a vantage point where he can watch what people are giving. There in the Court of the Women, against the wall, were 13 trumpet-shaped brass receptacles for collecting offerings.

As people give, He notes both the offering and the heart behind the offering. He counts the dollar bills and change. He reads

Day Fourteen—Mark 12:41-44

the amount on the checks. It's as if he were to follow each usher this morning and watch what everyone puts in.

What do you think of Jesus sitting here, watching what people give? He watches the rich as they threw (lit. kept throwing) in large amounts. The idea is that the rich came and in some prolonged act they repeatedly cast their money into one of 13 large trumpet-shaped receptacles in the courtyard of the women. They pulled out their wad and in some pedantic way peeled off a large portion, one by one. Actually, there was no paper money or checks, so you hear the clang of the large gold coins as they hit the brass receptacles.

Then along comes a widow, a woman who is somewhat disadvantaged in society because she has been bereft of her husband. She appears to be alone. She is not only a widow; she is a poor widow. She's destitute. She's probably dressed in a beggarly fashion; she's thin, suffering from malnutrition; she's a bit unkempt. She casts her money into the treasury—two lepta. You might have heard—clink, clink—two very small copper coins, worth only a fraction of a penny. (two lepta—a lepton was a copper coin worth 1/128 of a denarius—a denarius was the average daily pay of a laborer. Two lepton equal 1/64 of a denarius—1/64 of the daily pay of a laborer—barely enough for a whole loaf of bread.)

Jesus observes all of this intently.

He is also aware of the shameful irony that a poor and destitute widow is living among the people who were to bless the nations and who were to have special care for the poor, widow, orphans, and strangers.

He is aware that the plight of this woman is due to the neglect of the religious leaders and the people and that perhaps even through the criminal acts of Scribes who often with a stroke of the pen would steal a widow's estate and leave her impoverished.

It even gets worse. Jesus not only knows what the rich folk and the widow gave, he knows what they kept for themselves. He later says that the rich gave out of their wealth; the widow gave out of her poverty. He knew that rich could dine in a fine restaurant after they left the temple; he knew that the widow had no idea from where her next meal was coming.

Poetic Meditations on Selected Scripture

It is important to note what Jesus does not say about her giving. The temple, though facing impending destruction, is still the symbol of worship to the living God. It is corrupt, unjust, exploiting, etc. Yet for this woman, it is still the place of worship. Jesus does not question why a destitute woman would give to an institution that exploits her in her poverty. Not that he approved, but that is not his point. His point is that there is something about this woman in her humility, simplicity, sincerity, and generosity that highlights the gospel and discipleship. In the midst of what has become a corrupt religion, there is still true faith.

HOW MUCH SHALL I KEEP FOR MYSELF

Ragged, unkempt, and beggarly was she
Alone, bereaved, in poverty
Two pennies was all she had to give
She had nothing left in order to live

She came to the temple ready to pay
Not caring for life beyond that day
Trusting in God knowing He's kind
Believing in Him, peace she would find

Giving is something that comes from the heart
Whether giving it all or giving a part
My giving says a lot about me
It displays a love that Christ can see

He knows true giving, for He gave his all
It's not the size whether great or small
True giving answers the question—why?
Why would the Son of God suffer and die?

He died so that we could really live
In dying he showed us how to give
Like a widow who gave not just a part
But a widow who first gave her heart

Day Fifteen—Mark 13:1-13

Will I Stand True to the End?

Jesus talks about the future and its dangers in order to call the church to watchfulness and vigilance. He offers no help in being precise about dates and times. He warns about false prophets who use cataclysmic world events to create hype about the end. He makes it clear that no one knows the day or the hour. He likens the trouble that comes to this world as birth pains, i.e., contractions. Birth pains indicate a birth will take place but the birth pains offer no precision about the time of birth. At times the birth pains may be false contractions or the pain may lead to prolonged time of labor.

In some sense Jesus' words are not very comforting. He tells us of the kind of treatment his friends and followers can expect in a fallen world. Yes, we find comfort in thinking of his glorious kingdom and of heaven and of a blissful eternity with Jesus. We also find joy in knowing that we've received eternal life through faith in Jesus Christ. However, we often have illusions about the kind of life that we should have before the birth of the New World. Somehow, we think that we should avoid labor pains. I know of no woman who loves labor, however, those who love the joy of birth are willing to endure the pain of labor.

"Enduring to the end" is being faithful unto death. There is no promise of deliverance from suffering and martyrdom. The promise is that, if and when death comes, salvation belongs to those who endured. Now we know from Scripture that salvation is God's gift received by faith in Jesus Christ. What does persevering have to do with faith and eternal life? The teaching of Scripture is that perseverance is a fruit of true faith.

We are called to endure till the end—whether the end is natural death, martyrdom, or the coming of Christ. Will you endure for Christ? Will you face the reality of suffering? Will you be faithful to his name? Will you demonstrate by your perseverance that your faith in Christ is genuine? Will you be faithful to your friend and Savior, Jesus?

TRUE TO THE END

A few more trials, a few more tears
Trouble comes for days and years. . .
Yet true is His promise for all that believe
Eternal life his children receive

He's my friend, this I won't deny
He's my brother; always standing by
Though by many, he's severely hated
Denying him is not contemplated

To me He's the deepest joy of my heart
To others he stirs fear from the very start
I smile at his awesome beauty and grace
While they have eyes full of disgrace

I pray when called to suffer for His name
I'll faithfully stand and not die in shame
My broken life, such a small price to pay
As I look at His grace that showed me the way

Yes, a few more trials, a few more tears
Trouble comes for days and years. . .
Yet true is His promise for all that believe
Eternal life his children receive

Day Sixteen—Mark 13:32-37

Choosing to Live in the Real World

Any world in which you live, whether it's a computer-generated world, a mind-generated world, a drug-generated world or a self-generated world is a world of virtual reality, if it leaves Christ out (Eph 2:8-10). It is possible that you and I can live in a world that we've created but in actuality is not the real world of fulfilling God's purposes for our lives. If who we are in Christ and anticipating the coming of Christ do not influence all that we do in everyday life, we end up living in a temporal self-created world rather than the world of eternal value. Living in a virtual world has consequences that affect you, those around, and your relationship with God.

In God's real world, people are gifted and assigned tasks. In God's real world people are loved and served. Those hurting are shown mercy. God's people are generous toward the needs of others. The gospel is preached among the nations.

The world of virtual reality is a world of self-gratification. No one is truly loved in a virtual world except oneself. No one has benefitted eternally in the real world by your living in virtual reality.

The real world is a world invested with gospel values. It is a world where people live with an eye to the Redeemer King. We look for Jesus because he is the Redeemer-King, the promised Messiah, the sacrifice for our sins, the only who saves and keeps us. The real world revolves around Jesus, i.e., "whatever you do in word or deed—do all in the name of the Lord Jesus" Any experience of life that leaves out the gospel is nothing more than virtual reality.

Poetic Meditations on Selected Scripture

Real life is entered through the gospel, nourished by the gospel, and centered in the gospel.

Sometimes we should pinch ourselves spiritually to see if we are awake and ask certain questions!

1. Do I experience joy in knowing that in Christ I have everything that my soul needs for eternity?
2. Do I look to him for daily grace to sustain me in the difficulties of life?
3. Do I forsake the idols of approval, comfort, and security because I am content in Christ?
4. Do I live with expectation and confidence knowing that Christ may return at any moment?
5. Do I care about the eternal destiny of those God's places in my path? Do I pray for them, love them, meet their needs, and talk to them about Jesus?
6. Do I spend time seeking God's will for my life wanting to invest my life for gospel values?
    a. Do I share the gospel value of loving people who are not like me?
    b. Do I share the gospel value of caring for the poor?
    c. Do I share the gospel value of generosity?
    d. Do I share the gospel values of seeking justice and mercy for the oppressed?
7. Do I love the people of God and encourage them to live faithfully?

CHOOSING TO LIVE IN THE REAL WORLD

We choose to live in worlds of illusion
Seeking escape from lives of confusion
Experiencing moments of serenity
Giving little thought to eternity
It may not be real, but it sure feels good
Living in a virtual neighborhood
Taking from people all that I need
Giving up nothing, fulfilling my greed

Day Sixteen—Mark 13:32-37

Though I often wonder if there is more
Listening briefly for a knock on the door

Am I asleep or am I awake?
Is my life real or is it a fake?
Am I alive or am I dead?
Why am I riveted to this bed?

An evil force, a hand over my eyes
Another hand muffling my cries
I want to arise, be free, and live
Yet Satan says, "God can't forgive"

The gospel calls in the middle of night
"Arise from the dead, wake up to new life"
Alive in Christ through a blood transfusion
Escaping the world of masked illusions

"Accept the task I've called you for
Be watchful as a servant at the door
Fix your eyes toward eternity
For knowing Christ is Reality"

Day Seventeen—Mark 14:22-26

A Promise that Can't be Broken

The New Covenant is sealed with blood. Jesus dies the death that covenant breakers deserve so they can experience the New Covenant.

In Genesis 15 Abraham expressed a need for assurance from God that God would truly bless him and his seed. In response to Abraham's need of assurance, in 15:9-21 Yahweh (or Jehovah as some would say) elevated the promise of land for Abraham and his seed to the status of covenant. First, Yahweh engaged in a ceremony that confirmed the inviolability of His covenant with Abraham and his seed.

In obedience to God Abraham gathered, divided, and arranged selected animals on the ground. In the darkness of the evening, Yahweh, in a visible manifestation of Himself, passed alone through the midst of the divided animals, thereby taking upon Himself an oath of self-malediction (Robertson 1982, 130). Normally in sealing a covenant both parties would walk through the dead carcasses swearing a similar fate to them if they failed to keep the covenant.

The significance of this ceremony lies in God's oath, wherein He solemnly swears death upon Himself should He fail to fulfill His promise to Abraham (Robertson 1980, 130-1).

What is striking is that Abraham and his descendants are the ones, such as we, who break covenant with God. We sin and we rebel. Yet the covenant maker instead of calling for our death, takes our death upon himself. Again, Jesus dies the death that covenant breakers deserve so they can experience the New Covenant.

Day Seventeen—Mark 14:22-26

The New Covenant is also redemptive. It secures salvation for those in Christ. The New Covenant restores all that was lost to fallen humanity. Every time we raise the communion cup we affirm, "I am saved, purchased by the blood of Jesus Christ. I am forgiven."

The New Covenant also anticipates the eternal kingdom. Our regular celebration of the New Covenant in Christ anticipates the day when He will share the cup with us in His Kingdom. Imagine that day!

It is not by accident that Jesus speaks of the New Covenant at the time of Passover. The Passover celebrated Israel's redemption from Egypt and also anticipated that God's people would enter the kingdom of God.

Every time we raise the cup, we affirm that we look for the day when we will share the cup with Jesus in his kingdom.

A PROMISE THAT CAN'T BE BROKEN

He made a covenant with me
A bond, a promise eternally
Words not casually spoken
Vows which cannot be broken

A covenant of sins forgiven
A promise of life in heaven
A vow to hide me in His love
A sure word from heaven above

My part is only to believe
Through faith his promise I receive
His blood, an indelible seal
Affirming God's promise is real

I rest in His covenant with me
His promise is mine eternally
His words are not casually spoken
His Vows can never be broken

Day Eighteen—Luke 2:10

Great Joy

Let's confess that we all have lost the great joy of the gospel at times. How we wish we could go back and have the gospel redeem those situations where we failed to have great joy.

How about that instance when you spoke cruelly to your spouse? How about those times when you disciplined your children in anger? Don't you wish that the great joy of the gospel had redeemed that situation so that you might have been kind and forgiving? Can't we all remember times when we knew we were right; yet our hearts were wrong and our words were wrong? Oh, if only we had been conscious of the gospel and its power to redeem every situation in life. We would have and still can heal those broken relationships!

We have much difficulty in experiencing the great joy of the gospel because the flesh would rather work than believe. In some sense it is easier to work it out ourselves than to rest in the gospel. When the gospel does not inform all of sin-affected situations, the result will be bitterness, resentment, evil speaking, and malice. With these things the Spirit is grieved! When the Spirit is grieved there can be no great joy

Today we need to turn back in faith in the gospel and allow the joy of the gospel to redeem those situations in our lives filled with bitterness and to redeem those broken relationships that cause anguish in our souls.

There's nothing like the joy of a new believer. Whether they were struggling under the burden of religion or captured by the power of sin, when they hear that God took on human flesh to save them, that

Day Eighteen—Luke 2:10

eternal life is a gift, that their salvation is already accomplished at the cross, and that all they must do is repent and believe, there is great joy! "I once was lost, but now am found, was blind, but now I see."

I'm afraid that even though we know the gospel we sometimes fail to see the emptiness of religious activity. Our joy is not in what we do, but in the gospel.

These shepherds were likely numbered with the few in Israel who had a proper view of sin and expected a Messiah who would deliver them.

These shepherds were conscious of their own sinfulness. Many believe that they were tending the sacrificial lambs to be used in the temple sacrifice. Those lambs were reminders to them of human sinfulness and the need of an innocent substitute to suffer death in behalf of the guilty.

These shepherds were aware of their lack of great joy. They saw the 1500 years of Jewish history since the law as proof that no one by keeping the law can live up to God's righteous standard; they saw that all men sin and fall short of the glory of God; they saw that external religion did not change a sinner's heart.

The self-righteous religious leaders did not hear the announcement of the Savior's birth. They did not believe the bad news about themselves so they would not appreciate the news of great joy. The shepherds had greater capacity to experience great joy because they accepted their human sinfulness and inability and helplessness.

GREAT JOY

Joy to the world, the gospel brings
Eternal life, my soul sings
A Savior, a King, a Mighty God
From golden streets to earthen sod

God in flesh, a mysterious union
Creator and created in close communion
Son of God and Son of Man
Fulfilling God's eternal plan

Poetic Meditations on Selected Scripture

Without sin, though bearing sin
Always good and pure within
Faithful, obedient and humble was He
Rejected, beaten, crucified for me

Joy to the world, the gospel brings
Eternal life, my soul sings
Of Peace, Joy and Life in the Son
Of Freedom, of Heaven, a Victory won.

Day Nineteen—Luke 19:41-44

His Tears

Jesus spoke these words at the time of His Triumphal Entry into Jerusalem. Palm Sunday is the traditional celebration of that entry. Five days later, the same person who was acclaimed as a king was crucified.

As Jesus approached the city, he looked over it from an elevated point on the Mount of Olives and he began to weep. Imagine this picture of Jesus weeping over the city while crowds are "joyfully praising God" (19:37) over his entrance as king. This was actually a sad day in the life of Jesus Christ! Why the difference of emotion? The people are rejoicing and Jesus is weeping!

At this point in history, Jerusalem is the territory of the Roman Empire. The Jews expected that their Messiah King would free Jerusalem from foreign tyranny and oppression. However, their rejoicing is short-lived because in the next five days, they will see their Messiah King bludgeoned and crucified.

The Jews of the 1st Century thought that the key to the peace of Jerusalem was power. Not a lot has changed in the 21st century in regard to Jerusalem's struggle for peace today.

There was rejoicing on at that Triumphal Entry because the people believed that Messiah Jesus would exercise the power needed to free Jerusalem from foreign domination. But, Jesus weeps while they rejoice! Why did Jesus weep over Jerusalem? Why does he weep over Jerusalem today? Does he weep over us for the same reasons?

Jesus implies that the city of Jerusalem should have known better in what to expect of the Messiah. He says very emphatically, *you, even you, should have known.* Now God has hidden the truth from them.

The occupants of Jerusalem made a fundamental mistake throughout history that continues to be made today. The mistake was that somehow land possession and relationship with God were equal, i.e., to have Jerusalem was to have God's favor. Though there was a relationship between spirituality and geography in ancient Israel, that relationship was never one of equality. God was always most interested in the condition of the human heart rather than the occupation of the land.

We make the same mistake when we say, things are going good in my life so God must be pleased with me, regardless of the state of my heart.

HIS TEARS

Why do tears flow down the face
Of the One who hung the stars in space
How can there be a broken heart
In the One who gave the world its start

The tears he sheds are tears for me
As He looks upon my tragedy
His broken heart and weeping eyes
Watch me love the sin I should despise

Amazing grace how can it be
What love that He should cry for me
Not only was it tears he shed
From thorns and spikes my Savior bled

His tears and blood flow for my sin
My life, my soul he died to win
His heart was broken, now mine's restored
He calls me friend; I call Him Lord

Day Nineteen—Luke 19:41-44

At times the tears flow down my face
As I think of his amazing grace
For he died with broken heart for me
His tears and blood brought victory

Day Twenty—John 1:1–20

Follow the Lamb of God

In the incarnation the Son of God acquired a human form and a human nature without change in His divine nature and personality. Jesus remained one person with two natures. Just as there is a mystery in understanding the Trinity, there is a mystery in understanding that Jesus is both Perfect God and Perfect Man.

The fact that He became flesh means that the Son of God took on a corporeal, material, tangible, and visible form of humanity, identifying with us in our humanness, not our sinfulness. Taking on human form means addition of human nature, but no subtraction of divine nature. In His incarnation, he remains as the eternal Son of God. He is both immanent and transcendent.

In eternity past, the Holy Trinity experienced complete satisfaction in the glory which they shared together. The glory of God is the awesomeness of His character, the brilliance of His majesty, and the infinite perfections of His being. The glory they shared together as the Triune God was sufficient for them. However, they delighted in creating the world and humankind so we can see the glory of God. It is this glimpse of the glory of God that brings satisfaction and sufficiency into our lives.

Somehow in all that is happening in your life, God wants you to see His glory. Whether it's through the manifold gifts that He may bring your way or whether it's through the pain and suffering that God has providentially brought to pass—God wants us to see His glory. You can only see the glory of God through Jesus Christ. The death and resurrection of Jesus assure us that we belong to

Day Twenty—John 1:1-20

God—we begin to see His glory in Christ and are transformed. By seeing his glory we are assured that in Him we have someone and something of eternal value.

FOLLOW THE LAMB OF GOD

Come and see—this Lamb of God
In Human form on earth he trod
Both Son of God and son of man
Revealing God's eternal plan
Jewish Messiah, sacrifice and seed
Prophetic hope for this world's need

Follow Him and you will find
Real peace, new joy, a renewed mind
A friend, a brother, yet a king
One of whom you'll speak and sing
A story, a subject, a joy to share
A priest who will your burdens bear

Come and see, follow and find
He's ever merciful, always kind
Fully human, slain in our place
Perfectly divine, amazing grace
Incarnate Word, the life, the way
Come and See! Follow Him today!

Day Twenty-One—John 3:16

The Story of Christmas—The Immeasurable Love of God

What makes the love of God measureless? The infinite love of God is seen in the lack of loveliness in the recipients. God's giving defies explanation. He is perfectly lovely; we have no loveliness. We are not attractive to God, Yes, even "all our righteousness is as filthy rags." Why does God love you and me? There is no rational answer to that, i.e., someone can examine us for a lifetime and find no inherent reason why a holy God should love us. He loves those who have no loveliness!

The infinite love of God is seen in the uniqueness of the gift. The heart of the Christian message and the Christmas story is that God gave His one and only son. God gave His one and only son with whom he enjoyed the most intimate communion before the creation of the world (John 1:1–3); God gave His one and only Son through whom he created the world (Col 1); God gave His one and only Son who is the very image of the invisible God (Heb 1:1–3).

The infinite love of God is seen in the manner in which the gift is given. God's gift was prepared and given in an unparalleled manner. It's not just the 33 years of Jesus life on earth. The gift was planned in the divine council of eternity past. The gift was prepared throughout 4000 years of human history. The gift was fleshed out in time and space in 1st Century Judea. The gift keeps giving throughout time and through all eternity.

The infinite love of God is seen in the power of the gift to rescue from eternal damnation. God's gift is a gift with a mission, i.e., to reconcile fallen humanity to a holy God. This is not the offender giving a gift of appeasement but rather the offended one giving to the offenders—winning them with love. Jesus did not come into a neutral world in order to save some and condemn others, he came into an already condemned world to save some. When we think of the power of this gift to rescue from eternal damnation, how can we measure the love of God? If you don't know this infinite love of God, please place your faith in God's one and only Son who died for you. If you do know this love, thank him today. Thank him with your life. Thank him by telling someone about the infinite love of God.

WHAT IS THE STORY OF CHRISTMAS?

A virgin, the Spirit, a barren womb
A babe, a manger, a cross, a tomb
A throne, a scepter, the Trinity
Tell the story of Christmas for me

The father, the Spirit, the only Son
Creation, the fall, the devil won
A promise, a seed, a victory
Tell the story of Christmas for me

Despair, disharmony, and sin
Unlovely, alone, no peace within
God's love, new life, at Calvary
Tell the story of Christmas for me

A gift of mercy, a gift of grace
Eternal life, a prepared place
Forgiveness, cleansing, I'm free!
Tell the story of Christmas for me

Thank you, thank you for the Son
Thank you for a victory won
Thank you for life eternally
This is the story of Christmas for me

Day Twenty-Two—John 5

The Helpless

Jesus models in his ministry what the Great Commission is all about, making disciples as he goes. In Jesus' journey to participate in an unnamed feast he finds opportunity for ministry.

I do not know whether it was necessary for Jesus to pass by this pool where he would have to see people in suffering. I suspect that he chose this path unlike many of us who choose to avoid face to face contact with suffering.

I doubt that this man had many people stopping by to hold a conversation with him. How many beggars, homeless people, indigents, poor people, widows, orphans do we avoid in order to not face their suffering? We get accustomed to walking on the other side of the street or avoiding the path that leads to contact with suffering.

We are not told why Jesus picks this man and not one of the many others who were there. This again reminds of the mystery of redemption and election. Though we shouldn't conclude that the healing of this one man was an end in and of itself because John, the gospel writer, chose this healing as one of the seven miracles he will write about to prove that Jesus is the Christ.

The selection of this one man also reminds us that healing was not an end in and of itself. If healing was the end in and of itself then why not heal the many others who were there? Healing was a pointer to Jesus as the Messiah, even as our works of mercy serve to point people to the Christ who can redeem them from their sins.

Day Twenty-Two—John 5

All of our efforts of mercy serve a similar purpose—though our signs are not miracles, as such, but rather deeds of mercy and kindness and acts of love that point people to Jesus Christ.

The question Jesus asks about 'wellness' has the possibility of double meaning, as do the previous metaphors of 'thirst' and 'birth.' The word for *well* can mean physical wellness, or it can mean 'wholeness' or 'soundness' other than physically.

The answer to Jesus' question should be obvious on the physical level. Why is this man here by the pool that has a superstition of healing attached to it? It obvious that he wants to be well physically—who doesn't? Jesus will meet him on the level of physical need to eventually probe the deeper need.

The lame man responds to Jesus question saying that he has no one to help him. I imagine that this lame man thought about his need of help often. As the crowds passed by, he could only imagine what could happen if someone cared enough about him to wait with him and at the right time would get him into the pool. Even though the waters of the pool couldn't help him, the superstition was real enough to him. His longing for someone to help him was real enough to him. Nobody cared about this man in his helplessness. He was not only imprisoned in a body that couldn't walk; he was imprisoned in a life or loneliness and helplessness.

There is no indication of this lame man's conversion in this text. He encounters Jesus twice with no apparent decision. I guarantee you that he never forgot what Jesus did for him. I imagine that when the death and resurrection of Christ took place and the gospel was being proclaimed that this man and others came to faith in Jesus Christ because at one point in their life, they were helped by someone who cared.

THE HELPLESS

Pressed down and battered
Defeated and shattered
Hearts cruelly broken
Words rarely spoken

Poetic Meditations on Selected Scripture

No comfort around
False hope surrounds
Floods of new tears
Ghosts of old fears
Darkness pervades
Tarpaper shades
A voice in the room
Piercing the gloom
Life-giving words
Good news is heard
Jesus is risen
Sin is forgiven
Heaven is sure
Life evermore

Day Twenty-Three—John 9

The Marginalized

Throughout the Gospel of John, we are reminded that Jesus is a friend of sinners. He is a friend of family members and friends; he is a friend of the religious; he is a friend of the social outcast; he is a friend of the helpless and hopeless. This morning we see that he is a friend of the *marginalized.*

To be marginalized means that you are not accepted by the central part of a social group. In different societies people are marginalized for various reasons, some because of choices they make, others because of factors over which they have no control.

The poor are marginalized because they are poor. Indigenous women are marginalized in India and many third world and Muslim countries because they are women. Women in business in America are marginalized because they are women. African-Americans are marginalized in many dominant white cultures. People with AIDS are marginalized because of their disease. The disabled are marginalized because they are deaf, or blind, or physically limited. Pockets of youth culture are marginalized because of their lifestyle choices. The elderly often are marginalized because they are elderly. And we could go on and on.

Every society has pockets of people who are either ignored, forced outside the mainstream of society, or who make choices that result in their being on the periphery.

The effects of marginalization may be varied: Statistics tells us that the marginalized are subject to greater emotional and physical health risks; they are more vulnerable to exploitation; they are more prone to drug and alcohol abuse; the suicide rate is higher among the marginalized.

Here is a blind man, marginalized from birth. He is pushed to the periphery of his society through no fault of his own. He dies a slow death of isolation, rejection, poverty, and humiliation.

Perhaps you feel marginalized this morning because of race or gender or economics or other distinctions that set you apart from others. Have you considered the possibility that your pain and suffering are part of God's plan to make your aware of your need of His salvation?

We may argue against God's fairness of justice or goodness in allowing this man to suffer blindness from birth, but you will do so futilely to this blind man. He would argue that.his suffering opened his heart to God's grace and prepared the way for him to experience that grace.

We cannot always give a detailed personal explanation for the suffering that individuals face but we know that God is at work in this world with the purpose of "calling out of the nations a people for His name."

THE MARGINALIZED

Invisible in a world refusing to see
A world without ears to hear my plea
A lonely life in a cloudy mist
Who cares that I even exist

Living on the edge without a friend
Hoping that soon this life will end
A person is what I long to be
Invited back into society

I crawl into my cardboard shack
The cruel, cold ground upon my back
Deep within I wonder why
A diminished self begins to cry

Day Twenty-Three—John 9

My pain is more than I can bear
Where is God? Are you there?
Do you look into my eyes?
Can you hear my pitiful cries?

If in my pain I turn to You
Will you answer, Are you true?
Do you have a plan for me?
Open my eyes, let me see

Christ's love soothes the aching soul
His grace makes the wounded whole
He becomes a sinner's friend
He's always faithful to the end

A cardboard box, yet a home in glory
Amazing grace tells my story
Cruel cold ground, yet streets of gold
No longer alone as I grow old

Though invisible to men I may be
I'm known by God intimately
Though banished to the edge of society
I banquet with the King eternally

Day Twenty-Four—Acts 1:15-26

Judas in my Heart

When you see someone you love, make sinful and destructive choices, you experience brokenness of heart. Heartache is the price of love and the cost of caring for others.

I try to imagine the disappointment of the disciples as they heard of Judas' tragic suicide. His suicide comes not from a love of death but from his despair over life. His death was not a total shock to the disciples. They had observed a pattern in his life that sort of predicted a tragic end.

Nevertheless, they had spent three years together in ministry with Jesus. They sat together in the mountainside classroom with Jesus. They engaged in mission together under the authority of Jesus. They observed the greatest concentration of miracles ever to occur in one place at one time in history. Together they enjoyed this unique calling to be the apostles of Jesus Christ. Yet, now one of the twelve has hanged himself—only eleven are left.

As I read this story of the eleven apostles gathering together to choose one who would replace Judas, I am impressed with the commitment these 11 men had to the mission that Christ had assigned to them. It's as if they are saying, yes, a tragic thing has happened, but God's work must go on!

God's work goes on despite the real progression and power of sin. On the surface much seemed right about Judas' life. He was a follower of Jesus—one of the twelve chosen. He participated in the mission of Jesus. He was one of those who served the 5,000

Day Twenty-Four—Acts 1:15–26

and the 4,000 as they were miraculously fed by the miracle of Jesus' multiplying the bread.

I don't talk about Judas' fall today as one who stands on a pedestal of self-righteousness. Rather, I speak as one who knows the power and deceit of sin and as one who has often been at the precipice of falling only to be rescued by the grace of God. Bob Jones Sr. has said that "Every tragedy of human character comes as a result of a process of wicked thinking." Judas' defection was subtle not sudden.

If you watched closely, you might have seen some indications of his defecting heart. When the forgiven woman poured out expensive oil on Jesus' head and feet, He objected and infected the other 11 disciples with a complaining spirit. The gospel writer said that Judas felt the way he did because "he held the bag"—he had an inordinate concern over money. Ultimately the money issue leads him to betray Jesus.

How often envy and bitterness are at the root of betrayal. Perhaps Judas watched with envy the relationship that Jesus had with Peter, James, and John, and that John was called the beloved disciple.

When someone lacks faith in Jesus Christ—a faith which opens spiritual eyes to see—he will have distorted values. Jesus was betrayed by Judas for the price of the lowest slave. For 30 pieces of silver he traded, eternal life, fellowship with Jesus, his position as one of the twelve, a future ministry, etc.

The satisfaction of this reward was short-lived because the pleasure of sin is only for a season. Eventually his guilty conscience caused him to give the money back—but it was too late.

He sacrificed the permanent on the altar of the immediate. What of eternal value do you trade for moments of temporal self-indulgence?

When the power of sin is ignited and enflamed in one's life, when that sin is not extinguished by repentance, it will destroy like a wildfire. The front door of sin is like the entrance into a 5-star hotel, but the back door leads to a garbage dump. For every moment of laughter in sin there are lifetimes of pain and regret. For every smile in sin, there are a thousand tear drops.

Poetic Meditations on Selected Scripture

JUDAS IN MY HEART

Judas fell from an honorable place
That name speaks only of disgrace
Betraying the one who loved him most
He's doomed, and damned, forever lost

For thirty coins of tarnished silver
Forfeiting life that lasts forever
He sold the priceless Son of God
His silver bought a pauper's sod

His dirty deed brought deep regret
A sad and tragic end he met
His treachery caused a horrible death
Remorse and shame, his final breath

Can grief undo the dirty deed?
Though with great tears a man may plead
Can grief revive the One betrayed?
No tear can bring life from the grave

We all have done the Judas' deed
His heinous act we all agreed
His kiss, our kiss one and the same
His sin, our sin, we own the shame

To the cross Christ wore the traitor's kiss
Mingled with blood and sweat, all of this
Bloody thorns and spikes of shame
Until that final moment came

Our betrayals nailed Him to that tree
He welcomed the pain to set us free
A blood-soaked cross, a rich man's grave
He had one goal—traitors to save

His blood can cleanse a traitor's soul
From guilt and shame to be made whole
To a lover's heart and a lover's kiss
To resurrection joy and eternal bliss

Day Twenty-Five—Acts 2:22-38

Does it really Matter?

One of the common words of our culture is "whatever." It is the word that ends many discussions. It may mean—I really don't care or am not interested; it's not that important; I really don't have time for this; you really don't know what you're talking about, that's just the way you think, etc.

To be fair, "there are some things on the scale of importance that deserve a "whatever." Many things in life are a "whatever"—such as what you think of baseball or motorcycles.

For a psychologized culture "whatever" is often an escape from discussing the important issues of life. The Bible challenges us to have a love that keeps growing in knowledge and discernment so we can choose the things that really matter. There are some things that deserve more than a "whatever."

One problem with "whatever" is that we often neglect what really matters for the "whatevers" of life. Or some may live with such ambivalence that they relegate everything to a "whatever" status.

More often than not, "whatever" at its core is probably rooted in selfishness and pride. Frequently saying "whatever" is an act of rudeness. Often "whatever" is a declaration of self-importance because it says, "things only matter if I say they matter." "Whatever" often reflects an aversion to objective truth and objective importance, i.e. "things are true and important if I say they are."

The "whatever" attitude of early 21st Century American culture is reflected in the secular mind's attitude toward religious belief—"Spiritual issues don't matter unless I say they matter and when I say they matter—whatever."

Unfortunately, even among professing Christians, a "whatever" attitude pervades. "Whatever" is reflected in sporadic church attendance, in the absence of the habit of giving, in non-involvement in evangelism and missions. "Whatever" characterizes how husbands, wives, and children approach their God-ordained responsibilities in the home. Even when it come to the question of sin, the attitude is often "whatever."

Conversely, the Bible calls us to responses that reverberate with "Amen." The fact that the historical Jesus of Nazareth was the one appointed by God to die for the sins of the world deserves an "Amen" not a 'whatever." The fact that His resurrection and exaltation were foretold 1000 years before it occurred deserves an "Amen" not a "whatever." The fact that God has declared Jesus to be both Lord and Messiah deserves an "Amen" not a "whatever."

Faith in Christ and His words transforms a life of "whatever" into a life of "AMEN!"

DOES IT REALLY MATTER?

Whatever ,whatever, whatever
Who cares if I live forever
You know, I think, So What, Whatever
Truth changes like the daily weather

Some say Amen, others say whatever
Some say they know that they'll live forever
So what, who cares, I don't, whatever,
What really happens when life is over.

If Christ is dead, then say whatever
If He's alive, then it really matters
In a dying breath, there's no whatever,
Only fear of judgment and hell forever

Day Twenty-Five—Acts 2:22–38

God's grace converts a casual whatever
Into faith and life that lasts forever
An empty soul wants more than whatever
It needs a king to reign forever

Day Twenty-Six—Acts 3:12–26

The Gospel Satisfies

The occasion for the speech is the healing of the beggar and the questions that arose over this healing. The audience is composed of Jews who are astonished at the miracle that has just taken place (3:10–11). Peter uses the occasion to draw a connection between the God of Israel and Jesus, in whose name this beggar was healed.

Peter mentions two times that follow repentance and forgiveness, times of refreshing and the time for God to restore everything.

Peter's words address the two great realities of the Christian life—one is present and the other is future. The first reality we can call an experience of refreshing. We can call the second reality an expectation of restoration.

These two realties address two great needs of humanity—the need of relief while living in the midst of an oppressive world and the need of hope for restoration while living in the midst of a broken world.

Why do we need refreshing? We need refreshing because sin and the results of sin oppress the soul like the heat of the sun. What is this refreshing? Literally, it is relief from heat, like a cool breeze on a hot day. Figuratively, it portrays relief from distressing circumstances.

Coming to Christ is described as an experience of refreshing. This is what Jesus Christ offers to sinners "Come to me, all you who are weary and burdened, and I will give you rest" (Matt. 11:28)? The burden of the pilgrim falls off at the cross, and he is refreshed. No longer oppressed by the heat, he is breathing fresh, cool air; no

Day Twenty-Six—Acts 3:12-26

longer parched with thirst. He is drinking the cool, refreshing water of life that only Jesus Christ gives.

Why do we need restoration? We need restoration because sin breaks and destroys and in every soul is the longing for its brokenness to be healed. The Jews longed for the day of the Messiah when their Humpty Dumpty world would be restored. Remember that little rhyme that is so full of good theology.

> Humpty Dumpty sat on the wall,
> Humpty Dumpty had a great fall:
> All the king's horses and all the king's men
> Couldn't put Humpty together again.

Only the Messiah can restore the world. So Christians live with no expectation of complete restoration apart from the coming of Jesus Christ. We are realistic about depravity, sin, Satan, the curse, a fallen world, etc. We live with hope. The gospel has brought us hope. We have tasted the glories of the age to come but we yearn to drink fully and completely.

THE GOSPEL SATISFIES

> Souls cries out for refreshing
> Parched by their sin and pride
> Longing for fresh anointing
> Running out of places to hide
>
> The soul's deep need is repentance
> Turning from sin and despair
> To know the joy of forgiveness
> The Spirit-wind breathes cool air
>
> The gospel, a cool mountain stream
> Flows gently o'er the desert soul
> What once was a feint dream
> Now the joy of a heart made whole

Poetic Meditations on Selected Scripture

An empty tomb, a blood-stained cross
Beckon to hearts filled with strife
Forgiven and spared from eternal loss
Drinking from the water of life

Yes, come and drink all who thirst
The fountain's open; it's wide and deep
Seek the Lord; yes, seek him first
He promises your soul to keep

The gospel flows in boundless streams
Refreshing every believing heart
The Spirit's work exceeds all dreams
If we believe, as at the start

Day Twenty-Seven—Acts 5:29-31

I Pledge Allegiance to the Gospel

Every Christian needs to ask, "How does the gospel transform my view of what it means to be patriotic?" Did Peter and the apostles love their country? Were they patriotic in any sense of the word? Why were they disrupting the status quo? Was not the history of the nation of Israel to be honored and perpetuated? How did the gospel alter Peter's view of patriotism?

As we listen to Peter's response in these verses to this religious/political body, we see that his understanding of the gospel had fundamentally altered his view toward what it means to be a good Israelite.

Even in the face of death, Peter does not struggle with his new sense of patriotism that goes against the status quo while offering them life in the gospel! Why not? Here are some suggested reasons:

1. He knew clearly what God had commanded. Peter's actions are not only driven by the personal revelation to preach but by the initial command in Acts 1:8. Acts 5 is a confirmation of the need to obey Acts 1:8 even in the face of opposition.
2. He knew the priority of the advance of the gospel. That fact that Jesus died and rose again and was now exalted permeated Peter's thinking. He was appointed to be a witness and everyone who has the Holy Spirit has this witness. This could not be separated from his love for his people.
3. He knew that the ultimate threat of death was not to be feared. He was willing to die for what he believed. When we think

about this, we narrow down what are the ultimate issues of obedience to God.

4. He knew that Christianity was not an immediate political threat to Rome. Peter would not have joined the Christian right. He did not see government as a means to advance the gospel of Christ. In medieval times popes and bishops abused these same words of Peter ("we ought to obey God rather than man") to force people to submit to Christianity. This was not Peter's intention.

5. He knew that ultimately the coming of King Jesus would destroy all earthly kingdoms. What is the destiny of the USA?—to be destroyed by the kingdom of the Lord Jesus Christ!

Peter was a different Israelite after he confessed Jesus as Lord!

I PLEDGE ALLEGIANCE TO THE GOSPEL

Yes, on this day
The U S A
Is worthy of some praise
This is our nation
Unique creation
Blessed in many ways

Nations rise
They face demise
His Kingdom stands forever
A holy nation
His new creation
Naught from Him can sever

This is my choice
To lift my voice
For Christ who died for me
I pledge my all
I've heard His call
To life and liberty

Day Twenty-Seven—Acts 5:29–31

He is my king
To Him I bring
A life that seeks His glory
A stranger here
The goal is clear
To tell redemption's story

No earthly place
Can e'er displace
The passion for my King
All other loves
Are lesser loves
Of Jesus I will sing

Day Twenty-Eight—Acts 15:1-21

Free in the Gospel

There are two interrelated questions in this text. What is the core of the gospel? The answer to this never changes. How do I live my life? The answer for 1st century Gentiles in Antioch Syria is not the same for those living in the 21st Century, though the principles are the same.

First of all, live in a way that promotes unity among believers. He is not using the argument of law but the argument of love for your brother and love for the lost. It is a gospel-centered argument not a legalistic one. James is not here laying down a law but calling Gentiles to loving consideration. Later Paul will develop theological arguments that clarify that anyone who believes that eating meat sacrificed to idols is wrong is actually a weak brother because an idol is an "non-entity." The four things he mentioned are all in a similar category of ceremonial uncleanness—the ritual defilement of idols, of sexual immorality, of strangled things, of blood.

James is referring to Gentile practices that prohibit Jews from involvement with Gentiles because they would be considered 'unclean' from an OT perspective. Even though the ceremonial laws of uncleanness are abolished in Christ (as Peter learned in Acts), Gentiles, in this early stage of the church, are called to defer to the weak consciences of their Jewish brethren.

The weak Christian in Scripture is normally the one who has a cultural list of taboos and judges the spirituality of others by it. Gentiles are to consider Jewish sensibilities toward ceremonial uncleanness for purposes of evangelism and fellowship with Jewish

Day Twenty-Eight—Acts 15:1-21

Christians with weak consciences who still have the Law of Moses affirmed to them.

At this point in their becoming Christians, they hadn't made a clear break from Judaism, though that would come as the writing of Hebrews makes clear. These Jewish Christians still did not grasp how Christ fulfills the law of Moses in all its aspects and that the law of Christ is the law of love that brings liberty not bondage.

Secondly, we live in a way that doesn't obstruct the gospel. Our commitment to the gospel determines whether we go beyond our comfort zones at times or restrain our liberty at times!

For instance, it may be something as simple as living in a neighborhood where people take great pride in their property. For you to disregard that and not care for your own will mean that you will close the door to a credible witness. We must be sensitive to both church culture and secular culture for the sake of the gospel—not so much to one's own private cultural views of how life should be lived, i.e. we don't need to defer to every person's peculiarity about life—"I'm offended because you don't have a tie on or because you eat meat."

If you are the type of Christian who demands that others jump through many hoops before they can be accepted by you—this text calls you back to a fresh understanding of the gospel.

If you are a Christian who enjoys an unabashed freedom in Christ, then understand there are weak Christians with deep sensibilities (right or wrong) that you must consider.

This text calls all of us to come to the glorious liberty of the gospel of Jesus Christ and the grace and love that flow from that gospel. I have often likened riding a motorcycle to living the Christian life in that it takes a special discipline while offering an unparalleled joy. Were you to pass me some day coming the other way, you might look and see a big smile come across my face. I've probably just said, "thank you Lord for your grace."

Poetic Meditations on Selected Scripture

FREE IN THE GOSPEL

Eyes on the road
Twilight emerging
Whispering Wind
Sunset behind
Night and day converging

Refreshing cool breeze
A Breath of freedom
Fresh blooms of flowers
A new moon this hour
Goodbye to boredom

Thoughts of Christ
The giver of blessing
Secure in his grace
A Smile on my face
His name confessing

Day Twenty-Nine—Romans 1:1–7

He's Alive

One thing that's interesting about these seven verses in our English translation is that they comprise only one long, complex, yet coherent verse in the original language. In one sentence we are given an overview of the history of redemption and the purpose and meaning of life.

These verses tell us of the connection of the resurrection to God's mission to redeem lost humanity. The resurrection is theological because it tells us something about God's plan and purposes throughout history; the resurrection tells us something about Jesus Christ; the resurrection tells us something about the need of the world and humanity.

What you believe about the resurrection determines what you believe about the power of God, about the death of Christ, and about redemption from sin.

According to Paul's discussion in 1 Cor 15, if the resurrection has no theological meaning to you, then you simply are not a Christian. The resurrection is a life-changing event. Paul was called and transformed by the living Christ.

Paul could well remember that day on the Damascus Road when he met Jesus, risen from the dead, and experienced a transformation, a conversion, that literally 'set him apart' for the gospel.

Has your belief in the risen Christ and your coming to know Him radically altered the way you live your life? Do you remember a day, when you placed your faith in Jesus, who died and rose again? Are you consciously aware that you are in a relationship with

Poetic Meditations on Selected Scripture

someone who is alive and leading your life? Do you live with an awareness that, as the people to whom Paul wrote to in Rome, you are loved by God and called to be saints?

The resurrection is a life-directing event. Paul's mission in life was redirected by the living Christ. Paul could not disassociate his belief in the resurrection from a call to mission. It is a belief in the resurrection that propels Christianity outward. The resurrection is the impetus for all outreach and mission. Paul understood that the resurrection of Jesus initiates a call for people of all nations to believe in Christ and submit to His Lordship in obedience.

It is the resurrection that caused fearful disciples hiding behind locked doors to throw open those doors and declare to the world "repent and believe, for He's alive."

HE'S ALIVE

He's Alive; it's Him I Love
For me His throne he left behind
He's Alive; it's Him I Love
I am the wayward sheep he finds

He's alive; in Him I believe
He's Son of David, a king is He
He's alive; in Him I believe
The Son of God, eternally

He's alive; it's Him I obey
Appointed as Lord; He's given all power
He's alive; it's Him I obey
He's calling sinners to repent this hour

Day Thirty—Romans 6:23

A Gift of Grace

Many people think and many religions teach that no one can really know for certain that God will accept them. Their reasoning goes like this: How can I know that I've done enough good things for God to let me into heaven? Religion focuses on the word 'do,' i.e., follow these rules, obey these commandments, keep these sacraments, try your best, live a good life, and maybe at the end God will let you into heaven.

This verse tells us that our good actions cannot earn us life because our evil actions have already earned us death. Because we sin, we deserve death not life. Sometimes we think that we're really not that bad. But, think about this for a moment. If you were a really good person you might sin only three times a day. If you're thirty years old that means so far you have sinned over 30,000 times. Can you imagine standing before God today and saying, "Please let me into heaven because I've only broken your law 30,000 times?" If you think about it, you really don't want God to give you what you deserve, because we all deserve death for our sins.

Eternal life is a gift that we receive by asking in faith; it is not something we earn or deserve. My wife gave me a ring for our 30th wedding anniversary. I didn't ask her how much I needed to pay her for that gift. She paid for it! Someone gave me a gift one day and I asked him if I owed him anything. He said, "Don't insult me." We insult God when we try to earn what he wants to give us. He paid for this gift through the death of his Son.

Think about this for a moment. When Jesus died, He died the death that you and I deserve because of our sins. He can offer us eternal life because he already suffered the death that we deserve.

You can know that you will live with God forever only if you have received his gift of eternal life. You don't deserve it and can never pay enough for it, but it can be yours simply by telling God that you need and want that gift.

In September of 1970 someone told me about that gift and helped me pray to receive it. Today I would like to help you to receive that gift by praying this prayer:

Dear God, I know that I am a sinner. I cannot save myself. I believe that Jesus died for me and rose again. Today I ask you to forgive my sin. Please give me the gift of eternal life. Thank you for that gift. From this day forward help me to live my life for you. In Jesus name, Amen.

A GIFT OF GRACE

Gift-giving is an expression of grace
Coming from hearts where yet is a trace
Of fallen humanity, sin, and depravity
A longing, a passion, a quest for eternity

We give 'cause we're made in the image of God
But a path of rebellion we all have trod
Yet within persists a feint recollection
Of being created in joyful perfection

A small bit of grace implies there is more
If sinners give, what does God have in store?
His well is deep; His heart overflows
He's full of grace; He wants us to know

His giving rises to the highest height
A look at the cross will capture your sight
Of the Son of God hung in your place
Giving Himself, your gift of grace

www.ingramcontent.com/pod-product-compliance
Lightning Source LLC
Chambersburg PA
CBHW071737040426
42446CB00012B/2384